DANGEROUS MAMMALS

AFRICAN WILD DOGS

NorwoodHouse Press

Kim Thompson

Cataloging-in-Publication Data

Names: Thompson, Kim, 1970-.
Title: African wild dogs / Kim Thompson.
Description: Buffalo, NY : Norwood House Press, 2026. | Series: Dangerous mammals | Includes glossary and index.
Identifiers: ISBN 9781978577497 (pbk.) | ISBN 9781978577503 (library bound) | ISBN 9781978577510 (ebook)
Subjects: LCSH: African wild dog--Juvenile literature.
Classification: LCC QL737.C22 W555 2026 | DDC 599.77096--dc23

Published in 2026 by
Norwood House Press
2544 Clinton Street
Buffalo, NY 14224

Designer: Rhea Magaro

Photo credits: Cover, pp. 1, 16 Henk Bogaard/Shutterstock.com; p. 6 Jez Bennett/Shutterstock.com; p. 7 Nagel Photography/Shutterstock.com; p. 9 Rudi Hulshof/Shutterstock.com; p. 10 Wirestock Creators/Shutterstock.com; p. 11 charles Hopkins/Shutterstock.com; p. 13 Samuel Cox Photography/Shutterstock.com; p. 14 Richard Juilliart/Shutterstock.com; p. 15 Lars Royal/Shutterstock.com; p. 18 Cheryl Jayaratne/Shutterstock.com; p. 19 Bruce Crossey/Shutterstock.com; p. 21 Wandering views/Shutterstock.com

Printed in the United States of America

CPSIA compliance information: Batch #CWNHP26: For further information contact Norwood House Press at 1-800-237-9932.

TABLE OF CONTENTS

MEET THE AFRICAN WILD DOG

African wild dogs live in forests and grasslands on the continent of Africa.

These **mammals** are also called African painted dogs or Cape hunting dogs.

African wild dogs have tall, bat-like ears. They have colorful **coats**. No two dogs have the same patches and markings.

The white tips on their bushy tails can be seen from far away. The tips may act like flags to help the dogs find each other.

An African wild dog is about the same size as a German shepherd. Males are heavier than females.

African wild dogs are very **social**. They live in packs. Packs may have as few as five dogs or more than 20.

All dogs in the pack work together to hunt and care for babies. Each pack is led by an **alpha** male and female.

African wild dogs can run as fast as a car on the highway. They keep up this speed while chasing **prey** for long distances.

FAVORITE FOODS

African wild dogs are excellent hunters. They catch their prey more often than lions and leopards do.

They are so successful because they work together in packs. They sneak up on prey and surround it. Then, they chase!

African wild dogs are **carnivores**. They eat whatever animals they can find and catch. This includes birds, rats, antelope, and warthogs.

STAYING SAFE AROUND AFRICAN WILD DOGS

Sometimes, African wild dogs hunt farm animals. This makes people think they are dangerous. But people threaten them more than they threaten us.

African wild dogs are **endangered**.
There are not many left in the wild.

African wild dogs do not hunt humans. But they will **defend** their packs from anything that threatens them. To stay safe, do not go near them.

GLOSSARY

alpha (AL-fuh): the leader of a group of animals; dominant in a group

carnivores (KAHR-nuh-vorz): animals that eat meat

coats (kohts): hair or fur that covers animals' bodies

defend (di-FEND): to protect someone or something from harm or danger

endangered (en-DAYN-jurd): at risk of disappearing forever

mammals (MAM-uhlz): animals that are warm-blooded, have hair or fur, and feed milk to their babies

prey (pray): animals that are hunted and eaten by other animals

social (SOH-shuhl): preferring to be around others instead of alone

THINKING QUESTIONS

1. What are other names for the African wild dog?
2. What do African wild dogs look like?
3. How do members of a pack help each other?
4. What do African wild dogs eat?
5. Why do some people think African wild dogs are a threat?

INDEX

ABOUT THE AUTHOR

Kim Thompson has been an animal lover ever since she was little. She loves to watch animals and photograph them, especially in the wild. She thinks that learning about animals can inspire people to take actions that help animals survive on the planet we share.